MW01251147

WOMAN'S WORD FOR IT!

BY

Cy DeBoer

CCC PUBLICATIONS

Published by

CCC Publications
9725 Lurline Avenue
Chatsworth, CA 91311

For information address:
CCC Publications; 9725 Lurline Avenue,
Newbury Park, CA 91311

Manufactured in the United States of America

Cover ©1997 CCC Publications

Cover/Interior production by Oasis Graphics

ISBN; 1-57644-066-4

If your local U.S. bookstore is out of stock, copies of this
book may be obtained by mailing check or money order for
$6.95 per book (plus $2.75 to cover postage and handling)
to: CCC Publications; 9725 Lurline Avenue, Chatsworth,
CA 91311

Pre-Publication Edition - 4/97
First Printing - 8/97

A collection of words from a woman's point of view. An illuminating book for misunderstood women and the men who misunderstand them.

**To Bruce,
Ryan
and
Whitney**

Take my word for it –

I love you beyond
definition!

THE **A** COLLECTION

Abundance — Hordes of men who part their thinning hair just above one ear and swoop it to the other side.

Accident — A child conceived long after your husband's vasectomy.

Accommodation — A very generous term if used in the same sentence with the Holiday Inn.

Accurate — Precise details which can ruin a good story.

Acme — Delivery truck you don't want to see arriving on your 25th anniversary.

Acquire — Hips, headaches, and the neighbor's kids.

Acrobat — Men like this quality in a woman. It appears much higher on their list than "good personality."

Active — Man who doesn't use the remote. (Hyper-active — man who gets his own beer.)

Activate — Installing an electrical charge in the cushion of the Lazy Boy recliner.

Adapt — Evolutionary requirement to live with a man.

Addict — Person who waits in a grocery line 40 people deep to purchase a Twinkie with a check.

Adjourn — What men do following a large family dinner. See nap.

Adobe — Cement-like texture of brownies overcooked in the microwave.

Adolescence — By observing this age group, Rod Serling developed his ideas for The Twighlight Zone.

Advantage — What a woman has when her husband has been "on the road" for six months.

Adventure — Walking into a Biker Bar in search of a designated driver.

Aesthetics — Of little concern to people with velvet paintings.

Affair — Looks good in movies, in real life your only offers come from the criminally insane.

Afford — The trick is getting your husband to work as many jobs as it takes to do it.

After — Refers to the downfall of your once perfect figure following childbirth.

Aggravate — Remove sports section from newspaper.

Afoot — What never stops growing on your teenage son's leg.

Agony — Reliving your past through your teenage daughter.

Agitate — Ability shared by washing machines and men.

Ahoy — Ineffective greeting for picking up women.

Aim — Absent in males from the age of three on.

Air-conditioning — Only when your menu takes flight and you are eating your barbecued ribs with mittens, will the waiter consider turning this down.

Albatross — Bird with uncanny resemblance to various in-laws.

Album — Dreaded coffee table entertainment when visiting an unattractive family.

Alfresco — Before taking a chance on this dining experience inquire of your hostess the drive-by shooting rate in the area.

Alibi — ALWAYS have this figured out before driving damaged car home. If stumped, try "A violent gust of wind blew my car into the wall at K-Mart."

Alien — The result of 48 hours in the delivery room.

Align — Overrated condition for tires only men seem to care about — women just want them to roll.

Alimony — Insist new husband begin an escrow account on wedding day so you can be sure he'll have it when *you* need it.

Alive — Extract a prenuptial agreement from spouse requiring him to behave in this manner when in the company of your family.

Alloy — Not an acceptable metal for engagement ring.

Allure — Can be accomplished with diamonds, furs, exceptional personal hygiene and written proof of a vasectomy.

Aloof — Bedroom demeanor of a closet-gay husband.

Alternate — Get one of these if "aloofness" continues.

Aluminum — Considered a precious metal to men who drink beer by the six pack.

Ambrosia — Food cooked by almost anyone else.

Ambulance — Excellent deterrent for unwanted dinner guests when parked in your driveway.

Ambush — Procedure kids and dog follow the minute they hear mom come in the front door.

Anyplace — Where you'd rather be than the gynecologist.

Apache — Snide warpaint remark a mom makes to her 15-year-old daughter as she leaves with friends for the mall.

Aphrodisiac — First Class plane tickets.

Apparition — Your husband at Tiffany's.

Apron — Waste of fabric for anyone who has a life.

Arctic — Zone which can easily be created by the lady of the house when the man of the house forgets her birthday.

Aristocracy — The life you know you were born to but surely there was a mix up in the nursery.

Arson — Excellent method to change the husband's mind when he says "we don't need a new house!"

Artificial — This applies to anyone with bigger breasts, longer nails and thicker eyelashes than yours.

Asbestos — Practical apparel for Grandma when blowing out her birthday candles.

Assassin — If this vocation keeps showing up on your child's aptitude tests, you may want to have a chat with his school counselor.

Assets — Should be itemized and used as the gift wrap for the engagement ring.

Asylum — Don't let Realtor convince your husband to purchase a vacant one as a "fixer-upper."

Atrophy — What happens to your inlaw's legs when they are staying at *your* house on *their* vacation.

Attack — Intense maneuver made on the Oreos during P.M.S.

Auction — Usually a poor turnout if people have *already seen* your furniture.

Autumn — The time in a woman's life when her boobs are falling faster than the leaves.

Avalanche — A Zone warning that should be posted on the front door of your freezer compartment.

Average — General appraisal of other people's kids.

Awkward — Uneasy feeling created by the discovery your skirt has been tucked into your pantyhose since your last trip to the restroom.

THE **B** COLLECTION

Babble — Irritating sound coming from husband while he's balancing the checkbook.

Bachelor — Unhappy misfit who blames his lack of commitment on the fact his mother is not available.

Baggage — Items of your husband's to pack if his picture appears on a dating service brochure.

Baffle — Asking your husband where the kids are.

Bagpipe — Due to necessity for hot air, men play this instrument more often than women.

Bailiff — Be slightly leery if this is the occupation of your future son-in-law's best man.

Bald — Most men in denial — see "Abundance."

10

Balsa — Wood used primarily in the construction of hotel room walls.

Banish — This order should accompany a divorce.

Banjo — Instrument in a dead heat with the accordion for "least likely to turn women on." Beware of unblinking children on front porches playing this instrument.

Bankrupt — Overreaction by the courts just because you fell a little behind on your Neiman's bill.

Banner — If you were ever Miss *Anything,* you must begin to deal with reality and discard these useless reminders of your past. Seek professional help if necessary.

Bargain — Everything you pull out of your shopping bag to show your husband.

Barnacle — Unsightly organism clinging to the stack of dishes in a bachelor's sink.

Barracks — Hotel room where "kids stay free!"

Barricade — Necessary precaution to keep the kids in their rooms until sunrise on Christmas morning.

Barter — Exchange ritual which takes place when trying swap your kids with the neighbor or any unsuspecting person over the age of twelve for a night out.

Baton — Device which single-handedly kept woman from being taken seriously for decades.

Baseball — Sport with a little too much crotch scratching to be considered "entertainment for the whole family."

Batch — Easier to spell than quadruplets.

Because — No longer an acceptable answer after age three. However, can be used on senile husband if he inquires as to why you've transferred all of his assets to your name.

Befuddle — Telling your husband you have decided to become a stay-at-home nun and the only requirement is celibacy.

Behave — Ridiculous request made of small children and old men.

Behead — Preferable treatment to what happened during an "Introductory" offer at the Beauty College.

Bellow — Form of communication commonly used by your family when they want you to retrieve something for them.

Berserk — Uncontrollable rampage by your two-year-old whenever he hears the word, "NO!"

Bewildered — Look on husband's face when you ask him whether you look better in the red silk suit or the blue knit dress.

Bigamy — The original time share concept.

Bladder — Much too small in woman to begin with and practically non-existent during pregnancy.

Blame — What mothers are awarded for everything from: " I don't have any clean socks" to "I can't find my homework."

Blink — Don't if you want to catch any of the foreplay.

Bondage — See "housewife."

Bore — Martha Stewart.

Book — You can't write one until all of your family is dead if they are the type that will sue.

Bonus — What you've already spent based on the rumor your husband might get one.

Bowling — The sport of choice for androgynous women.

Bridge — You'll worry more about having one in your mouth than crossing one.

Broom — Obsolete except as a means of transportation during P.M.S.

Brown — Color only men can relate to (with the exception of chocolate).

Bulimia — Bingeing preferable to purging.

Bumper — Most useful apparatus on a car.

Burn — Highly successful technique for getting taken out to dinner. Feign disappointment and add tears if necessary.

Bus — Yellow torture chamber if you are a "field trip" mom.

THE **C** COLLECTION

Cable TV — Proof God is a man.

Cadavers — Men on benches at the mall.

Caffeine — Voted "best over-the-counter drug."

Calm — Feeling which can only be obtained when under the influence of nitrous oxide *before* going to the dentist's office.

Calorie — Who's bright idea was this?

Castrate — Procedure which should be performed on all men whose pants reveal an unsightly crack when bending over. Also men with white belts.

Casual — To a man: shirt optional. To a woman: man optional.

Catch 22 — Marriage.

Cellulite — A French word meaning "hail damage."

Chafe — Irritating skin condition which results if one had to lay on bed to zip her jeans.

Charity — Sex *before* he takes you out to dinner.

Child-proof — No such thing!

Chin — Yet another feature highly prone to the influence of gravity as well as multiplying.

Chocolate — In dead heat with shopping for "most satisfying experience."

Chisel — A "must" kitchen utensil. It serves as great visual aid for removing food from pan and convincing your husband this might be a good night to "go out" for dinner.

Chronic — Your husband's breathing.

Circumcise — Provides strong argument God may be a woman.

Coherent — Not possible for a mother by the end of the day. Speaking of which, when is that exactly?

Compass — Necessary travel instrument since gas stations no longer pump gas, or give directions. However while you're there, you can do the weekly grocery shopping.

Composite — Upsetting police artist's drawing flashed on your TV screen which strongly resembles the phone repairman in your kitchen.

Consequence — What must be paid if you've left your husband home with the kids for more than an hour.

Conspicuous — The 2 for 1 dinner coupon your husband is fanning himself with during your big night out.

Convent — Marriage alternative you may have dismissed too quickly.

Contradict — Tactic used to keep conversation going in marriages which have lasted over 25 years.

Convene — What mothers with strollers do at 10:00 a.m. when the mall doors open.

Cope — Impossible without heavy medication.

Corsage — Unattractive waste of flowers. Worst offender: Huge mum adorned with glitter and a pipe cleaner formed into your initials.

Cosmetics — The only reason to look in the mirror in the morning.

Covet — The Commandment which requires you to be happy with your husband, but doesn't insist you put the telescope away that is pointed at your neighbor's husband's shower stall.

Cranny — First home.

Criticize — Use caution during love-making. A major contributor to impotence.

Credit Card — Best 3 inches of plastic ever invented.

Creep — Only guy brave enough to ask you to dance in high school.

Curb — Annoying piece of cement whose only purpose is to rub the whitewalls off your tires.

Cute — Highly over-used word. Women over age 21 really don't care to be referred to in this way unless they dot their "I's" with little hearts and insist on being called "Gidget."

Cyclone — Mysterious act of nature which devastates many homes every time the kids come home from school.

THE **D** COLLECTION

Dabble — Seek a second opinion if this is your surgeon's self-proclaimed commitment to medicine.

Dainty — This cannot be said of the birthing process.

Danger — Situation your family will be in if Prozac is ever taken off the market.

Dawdle — Frustrating speed of your child on the soccer field.

Debacle — All attempts to prepare a soufflé.

Debate — Congenital ability in all children.

Debonair— Last known man fitting this description was David Niven.

Debris — All that is left when Mom returns from her weekend "get-away."

Decadence — Sleep.

Decomposed — Requirement for left-overs before you'll even consider not covering them with ketchup and feeding them to the *other* members of your family.

Deep — Out-of-touch men use this adjective to describe Rambo.

Deity — What your husband considers himself if he remembers to brush his teeth before coming to bed.

Deluxe — Word often misused by car rental agencies regarding your upgrade from the Geo Prism to the Hyundai.

Dent — Tend to be more of these on your thighs than at an auto body repair shop.

Deplane — Opportunity to "accidentally" kick surly stewardess as she tells you good-bye through clenched teeth and winks at your husband.

Deposit — Banking document used only for scratch paper.

Despondency — Gloomy mood which can easily set in if you discover you are pregnant and your husband is sterile.

Detergent — According to TV advertising this is a very meaningful product in the life of every woman. If she can make gym socks white, her life has not been wasted.

Diamond — Needs no explanation. Crosses all language barriers.

Diet — Proof Satan exists.

Dilemma — Whether to serve the noodles that dropped on the floor to your dinner guests. If it is your own family, this word doesn't apply.

Disappear — Supernatural ability men have immediately following dinner.

Disaster — Broken microwave.

Doze — What men claim to be doing when they are snoring so loud in the recliner, the windows rattle.

Drag — Men's definition of how they got to the alter. Very funny.

Dump — Word which comes to mind as you pull into *your* driveway following a Parade of Homes tour.

Dungeon — Laundry room in the basement.

Dust — Should be declared an ecological insulator and its removal should be against the law.

THE E COLLECTION

Earthquake — What it will take to get your husband to remodel.

Easy — Unfortunately, this may be the office scoop on your husband's personal secretary.

Ecosystem — What is developing in the vegetable bin of your refrigerator.

Eight — Six too many children.

Elaborate — To sit down to eat lunch rather than leaning over the kitchen sink.

Elapse — The last 20 years of your life.

Elevator — Never get stuck in one of these with a Life Insurance agent — it will make you *wish* you were dead!

Elope — Common recommendation made by fathers of daughters as they approach eighteen.

Elude — Necessary maneuver when husband asks to see your checkbook register.

Emancipate — Women have no hope for this until the first house is built without a kitchen.

Embalm — Best chicken recipes suggest this prior to serving.

Embarrass — Easiest victim: Teenage daughter. Sit in middle of front seat when she is driving with her learner's permit.

Embroider — There is a minimum of 2,000,000 better things to do with your time.

Emcee — The mother's role on a family vacation.

Emerald — Gem which should automatically be given to a woman immediately after giving birth. A carat per hour of labor is the rule of thumb.

Emergency — Everything which comes after the shouting of the word "MOM!"

Emotion — Women hold a huge lead in this category.

Endangered — Obstetricians who recommend "natural childbirth."

Energy — Nostalgic feeling of well-being which doesn't return until the kids have left home.

Engrave — Your children's initials in the coffee table.

Enlarge — Happens to your rear end in dressing room mirrors.

Enormous — Size of a wife's list entitled "Changes I Would Like to See in My Husband."

Environmentalist — Meddlesome activist who has now given us the obligation to sort trash as well as socks. Thank you so much.

Envy — Women whose husbands don't own a recliner.

Erase — Concealing product which is more responsible for "cover-ups" than Watergate.

Erotic — Making love in the winter with your socks off.

Errand — Cannot be used in the same sentence as "quick" if accompanied by children.

Estimate — If you are the field trip mom, this is not a good idea when taking a "head" count before returning on the bus.

Esteem — Word you never thought about until your psychiatrist kept mentioning your lack of it.

Estrange — This can happen between friends if she discovers you are dating her husband.

Euthanasia — Merciful elimination of middle-aged men who wear "pinkie" rings and multiple strands of gold chains.

Evacuate — What must be done when a guy has occupied the bathroom for more than a half hour.

Evaporate — Must be what happened to the oil in your car. What's all this gibberish about a warning light?

Exaggerate — No point in telling a story unless you do this.

Exchange — Excellent method of perpetuating the shopping procedure indefinitely.

Excruciating — Very subjective. To a man: A flu shot. To a woman: taking care of a man with the flu.

Exercise — Love the outfits! Buy them, carry around a water bottle and check your pulse periodically — forget the actual exercising stuff.

Exile — Illusive dream for a mother. No one ever sends us away until the kids are out on their own.

Exorcise — Beginning at age two this should be a part of your toddler's daily routine. Try to find a Priest who will give group rates.

Exotic — Dining at Taco Bell instead of McDonalds.

Experiment — Living with someone "till death do you part."

Expert — In his own mind, the man you're seated next to at a dinner party.

Extravagant — Leaving more than one light on in the house at a time.

THE **F** COLLECTION

Fact — Not as reliable as "women's intuition."

Faint — Tactic used by both sexes to avoid changing someone else's kid's diaper.

Fake — Your best features.

Famine — When all the fast food restaurants are closed.

Famous — What you need to become before you're too old to do the "talk show" circuit.

Fanatic — A woman who irons her husband's shirts.

Fantasy — Everyone else's life compared to yours.

Fast lane — The one you are never in.

Faucet — Blonde who made messy hair fashionable.

Fault — This is always yours, you don't have to earn it — it's yours!

Felon — Troubling if your son's year book picture has this word and "Most Likely to Become" captioned below.

Fetch — As in "Hillary, go fetch me a Big Mac."

Fiberfill — Where was this stuff in Junior High when you were stuffing your bra with lumpy old Kleenex?

Fiction — Notion that cheerleading is a basic stepping stone toward success.

Firm — Only thing left in the house with this quality is the mattress.

Flame Retardant — The damn kitchen!

Flu — Illness which renders husband and children helpless. Wife/mother is expected to go on as usual. This is where the term "Walking Pneumonia" originated.

Fluke — Choosing the right husband the first time.

Forage — What kids do for hours with the refrigerator door open.

Forehead — Constant area of expansion for most men over 30.

Forgive — Requires flowers, jewelry and some very serious groveling.

Fortnight — 24 hours in a KOA campground.

Fragile — A word from the past . . . before the kids broke them all.

Frequent — Bathroom visits during pregnancy.

Friction — If sparks occur from your thighs rubbing together when you walk, look into a diet.

Frigid — Term used by inadequate men regarding the woman in their life because they've never learned the art of "thawing out!"

Frisk — If you are married to a policeman, don't be surprised if this is his idea of foreplay.

Frog — Obviously, Princess Di should have left well enough alone.

Frostbite — A condition you must have written proof of from your physician before your husband will allow you to turn up the heat.

Frugal — Men's denial word for CHEAP!

Frump — What Queen Elizabeth should list under *Occupation*.

Frontier — For a man, the laundry room.

Fungus — Mold which is being marketed under the misleading name of "truffle."

Funk — State many women find themselves in when they've discovered their children have grown up but their husband hasn't.

Futile — Attempt to have entire family look like members of the human race for an expensive portrait sitting.

THE **G** COLLECTION

Gag — Suppression techniques should be part of childbirth class curriculum.

Galley — Whimsical, nautical alternative to dreary synonym — kitchen.

Gallows — Remodeling plans being considered for kid's bedrooms.

Gamble — Relying on birth control devices.

Gap — What seems to be growing between you and your husband since he hired a young secretary who can't type.

Garnish — Sickness bag would be more useful than parsley on a plate of airplane cuisine.

Gasp — Painful sucking sound used in conjunction with chest clutching made by men who are unable to locate the remote control.

Geezer — Older version of your husband.

Geometry — Who cares?

Gelatin — Midwest food staple.

Genetic — An excuse for any physical or emotional quality you don't want to overcome. Blame it on your parents — your kids will.

Genuflect — Appropriate response to anyone willing to watch your kids for the weekend.

Germination — Science project taking place in your teenager's tennis shoes.

Geyser — First used by Wilma Flintstone as a bidet.

Giblets — Every Thanksgiving you tell yourself, "If I wanted to touch those things, I would have become a Pathologist!"

Gingham — Call off the wedding immediately if your fiancé suggests you wear his mother's wedding gown, which is made of this fabric.

Gladiator — Necessary skill for adult entering the play room at Burger King.

Glimpse — What you'd like to catch of your daughter's date.

Glow — Erroneous adjective used to describe a pregnant woman. The correct term is "sweat."

Glutton — Person who purposely goes to hospital cafeterias when other food alternatives are available.

Goal — It appears your husband, the eight-track cassette salesman, forgot to set one for himself.

Gob — Description of everything found in your kid's pockets after they've gone through the wash.

Goggles — Recommended for changing a baby boy's diaper.

Golf — The game that makes men forget they are married.

Gong — Should be installed in the seats at operas.

Goof — Have a heart-to-heart talk with your daughter if her fiancé's family repeatedly refers to him thusly.

Gossip — Can officially be listed as a second language for women.

Goulash — Beige clump of noodles and meat men strangely crave.

Gradual — Realization you're starting to sound just like your mother.

Grave — Welcome alternative to the Kirby salesman.

Gravity — Unkind act of nature which begins to win the battle around age forty.

Gravy — Can single-handedly create the onset of gravity prematurely.

Graze — Impact of wife's conversation on husband's mind.

Grenade — Cannot be trusted to clear a golf course on a Sunday afternoon, men tend to "play through."

Griddle — There are better anniversary presents.

Groin — Administer an assault to this area upon receipt of aforementioned gift.

Grub — NEVER get involved with a man who uses this word in reference to food unless you have a penchant for campfires, pork 'n' beans, outdoor plumbing and being referred to as "Missy."

Guillotine — Bedroom accessory which encourages marital fidelity.

Gust — Unexpected wind responsible for blowing your car into the vehicle stopped at the light in front of you. Don't overuse this excuse it only seems to work once or twice.

Gypsy — Excellent lifestyle choice for a woman who likes cheap jewelry and can't settle down.

THE **H** COLLECTION

Habitable — Men: Cot, TV with access to ESPN, a remote and a cooler of beer. Women: The Plaza, the Waldorf or anything with 5 stars other than a General.

Hack — Warning signal men give prior to spewing forth revolting, wet, gooey objects to the ground.

Hail — Act of God responsible for thigh dimpling — not cellulite!

Hair — Protein follicle which controls a woman's sanity.

Haggle — It can be unpleasant to discover your husband is engaging in this activity in order to find you a ride home from the party.

Hammock — Do not purchase this Father's Day favorite — it encourages a lifestyle of which you DO NOT want him to become accustomed.

Hamster — Rodent resembling your children when they've stuffed their cheeks with portions of dinner they intend to spit in the sink.

Hamstring — Football injury resulting from tight pants on not so "tight ends."

Handsome — ANY man who is willing to support your five children from your previous marriage.

Hankering — Women prefer men not use this term in place of "desire."

Hara-kiri — Japanese for Cesarean Section.

Harass — Phone calls made by people who can't pronounce your name and want to sell you aluminum siding for your brick home.

Hardy — Women who do their own ironing.

Harem — Ignore your husband's request for one unless you really need your "space."

Harlot — Woman whose bust measurement exceeds her hip measurement.

Harmony — Elusive state of being at a family reunion.

Harpoon — When your overweight husband's snorkeling experience is cut short by this weapon, it is an unfortunate case of "mistaken identity" that can put a damper on the whole vacation.

Hatchet — Set this utensil at your place instead of a dinner knife and watch the improvement in the kid's table manners.

Haunt — Your post mortem plans if your husband remarries someone in her twenties.

Heap — Laundry site which any good therapist would tell you to ignore.

Heckle — Might be considered poor taste to do this to the person giving the eulogy at your ex-husband's funeral.

Heel — Command screamed at your new Canine Obedience School graduate as you're being dragged face down on the pavement.

Hell — Free passes to a Hunting and Fishing Exhibition at your local arena.

Hermit — Polls indicate this to be the most sought-after occupation for men over 40.

Hex — Should be put on all people who abuse the Express Lane privileges.

Hint — Wearing a chastity belt to bed.

Hips — Small word for BIG problem.

Hiss — Unsettling sound coming from your son's closet.

History — Nowhere near as entertaining as Her-story.

Holster — Beware the woman who carries her glue guns in one of these.

Honk — Overreactive, hostile sound made by idiot in car behind you when the light turns green and you haven't finished lining your lips in the rear view mirror!

Hopscotch — Whimsical manner of getting through your teenager's room and avoiding life-threatening piles.

Hormone — Mind poisoning secretions which could turn Mother Theresa into a serial killer.

Hour — Every 60 seconds that passes when you are in the car with your kids.

Housewife — Confining term which has led to the popularity of malls.

Howl — Unnerving fanfare which comes from both construction workers and Werewolves.

Hump — Difficult to cover during swimsuit season.

Hunch — If you do have a hump, don't aggravate it by doing this.

Hunk — Measurement for chocolate and diamonds.

Hussy — Term frequently whispered by your mother-in-law in place of your name.

Hyena — Ancestor of the movie patron seated directly behind you.

Hypersensitive — Man who cries while watching *Deliverance*.

THE **I** COLLECTION

Idol — Seek foster care for your son if he refers to Charles Manson as his.

Igloo — Ideal home for men based on Public Service savings alone.

Ignore — Congenital ability of men and children regarding any obstacle of clutter in home which does appear to endanger them.

Immobile — The kids after you get them bundled up to play in the snow. Now if you could just get them to stay this way.

Impersonator — Man who shows up at the door with roses and claims to be your husband.

Impetuous — In most cases, the decision to wear spandex outside the privacy of your own home.

Implant — Do this with a small recorder in your husband's ear that plays subliminal gift suggestions.

Impose — Feel free to do this with your husband's mistress by asking her to do his laundry.

Impregnate — Never again!

Impression — Let your first one be your guide if your blind date honks out front for you and his vehicle looks like it is primarily used for hauling.

Impudent — Word used by '50s moms. More contemporary version is "smart ass."

Inbred — In a word: Clinton.

Incarcerate — Should be done with people who blow their nose at the dinner table.

Incapable — Nagging feeling about yourself whenever your mother visits.

Incapacitate — The removal of all chocolate and caffeine products from your home.

Inch — Measurement which is lied about more than any other by both sexes.

Incident — Annoying word which your mother-in-law uses in reference to your wedding.

Incognito — The Prince who is suppose to rescue you is obviously traveling in this manner.

Incoherent — Husband's response when wife says "I'd like to talk about us."

Incombustible — The kitchen, the laundry room, the Lazy Boy recliner and some breeds of cats.

Incompatible — Your family.

Incomprehensible — Your children sharing a backseat without the onset of tears or blood.

Inconclusive — Any evidence which points to you as the one who ate the entire chocolate cake. Hide the Midol or it might be used to incriminate you.

Inconsiderate — Your husband's expectation of lovemaking if you just changed the sheets.

Incredulous — Look on the kids' faces if you actually say "No!"

Indecent — Women who can wear swimsuits without the little skirts.

Indefinite — All of your plans since your first child was born.

Indent — Less alarming adjective to use about the front of your car than "totaled."

Independent — Eunuchs.

Indescribable — Childbirth. Otherwise you'd never consent to it.

Indispensable — Mascara and chocolate.

Indicted — Can get your day off to a bad start if the morning paper has your husband's picture on the front page with this printed below.

Indignant — Attitude of sales personnel if you dare to ask "Can you help me?"

Indiscriminate — Bowlers.

Indivisible — Men and television.

Indulge — Do this with a glass of wine every half hour during your turn to host neighborhood "play group." Time doesn't go faster but you don't really care.

Inedible — Wet bread.

Ineffective — Your husband's tongue in your ear when you are standing at the stove preparing dinner and four of the six kids are attached to your ankles.

Ineligible — All bachelors with an abnormal amount of ear hair, or who constantly insist on "going Dutch."

Inert — Condition of a man whose remote has just gone on the "fritz."

Inevitable — That the aforementioned man will die soon.

Inexcusable — When the woman you suspect of having an affair with your husband asks to borrow one of his favorite recipes.

Inexpensive — Big word for CHEAP!!

Infatuation — The look on your husband's face when he meets a woman who can cook.

Inherit — *Best case:* The family fortune. *Worst case:* The family nose.

Inhuman — When your husband stops your credit cards.

Injury — This may occur as a result of the above.

Inkling — Premonition that something is wrong when all the people walking behind you are snickering.

Instead — Refers to everything you should have done with your life.

Insufficient — Banks really need to develop more of a sense of humor about this.

Insult — Being told by son's girlfriend she hopes she can look as good as you if she lives that long.

Intellectual — Cannot be found at a Rambo movie.

Intercom — Waste of money. Your family will continue to scream to one another from the third floor to the basement.

Interpreter — Yet another job skill requirement of mom.

Interrogate — Must be done to discover who left the empty milk carton in the fridge, the empty toilet paper roll in the bathroom and the baby-sitter locked in the basement.

Interview — Unnecessary step when hiring a Nanny. The fact they even showed interest in the position after seeing the toll your children have taken on you should guarantee them the job.

Intimate — Requires a totally unavailable amount of time and energy.

Invalid — Man with a splinter.

Invisible — Dust, you ninny — just don't run your fingers through it or rearrange the knick knacks.

Invitations — Conspicuously absent from your mail box since a member of your family was featured on "America's Most Wanted."

Iota — Quantity of time it takes to open the Christmas packages you devoted the last six months of your life to shopping for and wrapping.

Irreconcilable — Your marriage if your husband insists you introduce him at parties as your son.

Irredeemable — Anyone who brags about their ability to take more money out of the collection plate at church than they put in.

Irregular — A woman who cleans grout.

Irrepressible — The urge to kill the person who has been standing in the fast food line in front of you for 30 minutes and when it's his turn to order, he has no idea what he wants.

Irk — Another word from the '50s. When was the last time you were "irked off" at someone?

Irritating — The sound of your husband's breathing after an argument.

THE **J** COLLECTION

Jackal — Your ex-husband.

Jackass — Your ex-husband's attorney.

Janitor — A paid housewife.

Jealous — How your mother described all the people who taunted you throughout your childhood. (e.g. "They're just jealous because you can smell better with your big nose!")

Jeopardy — Situation a nursing mother is in when the baby is cutting teeth.

Jerk — Husband's description of every driver other than himself.

Jezebel — Nickname your mother-in-law insists on calling you.

Jiffy — Beware the woman who uses this term, no doubt she's on drugs.

Jitters — Feeling which can overwhelm you when you wake up beside your new husband and you can't remember why you married him.

Jodhpurs — Can ruin your day if someone compliments you on wearing this style of pants when you aren't.

Juggle — What do a mother and a circus performer have in common?

Jumper — Probably should not be worn by women in their 70's.

THE **K** COLLECTION

Karat — Don't accept jewelry with this word misspelled (i.e. carrot).

Keg — Container of beer for men or concealer for women.

Kelp — Can be a low fat substitute for turkey stuffing at Thanksgiving.

Khaki — Color of pants nine out of ten men select every time they get dressed. Selection is based on their "Goes with everything" theory.

Kilt — Men would probably wear these more often if they were khaki instead of plaid.

King — Monarch status that you have no intention of letting your husband reach in *your* house.

Kitchen — Hell with a microwave.

Kodak — How your parents refer to all camera equipment. "Get the Kodak, Martha, we'll snap a shot of the kids."

THE **L** COLLECTION

Labor — Defies definition.

Lackluster — Demeanor of wife when husband suggests lovemaking just after she's put the triplets to bed.

Lag — Time between meals.

Lagoon — La husband's best friend.

Laminate — Furniture men insist "looks just as good as the expensive stuff."

Larva — Good rule of thumb to throw hamburger out if this sort of creature can be seen in a frenzy of activity in the package.

Lax — State of a man's bowels until the dishes are done.

League — For men: Bowling. For women : Junior.

Leap — Never get involved with a man who enters the room in this manner.

Lease — Try this instead of marriage.

Lecher — Neighbor with excessive gold chains and an unusual supply of Girl Scout cookies.

Lecture — Tiresome rambling such as the "money doesn't grow on trees" speech.

Legend — What you pray your teenage daughter has not become with the football team.

Leisure — Obviously the inventor of this type of suit didn't spend his "leisure" time wisely.

Lenient — Parents who must ask their children's permission before leaving the crawl space in the basement.

Leotard — One in a trillion women can get away with this look. The odds for men are only slightly better.

Leprechaun — If you marry one, make sure he's *standing* on a pot of gold.

Lethal — Purely subjective. What's lethal for one unfaithful husband may not be for the next.

Lethargy — This mood sets in around 5:00 p.m. when you know you should put dinner in the oven, but you feel more like putting your head in instead.

Levitation — Psychic power the family must rely on to retrieve things around the house when mom isn't home.

Librarian — Not a fast track career.

Limber — Intervene if your husband's prospective secretary lists this as a qualification on her resumé.

Linen — Ancient fabric created before it became unfashionable to look like you've been wadded up in a bag for two years. Caution: It always looks good on the hanger.

Linger — Check your oral hygiene if your breath does this long after you leave a room.

Lingerie — Only women who are single or having an affair actually purchase from this department.

Litter — Against the law outside the home, however housewife should carry orange trash bags and a long poker when she does her daily rounds.

Loony — Get a second opinion if your Neurosurgeon considers this a favorable post operative sign.

Lotto — May be necessary to work outside the home if this is declared as your spouse's primary source of income.

Luxury — Being alone in the bathroom.

THE **M** COLLECTION

Macabre — Kissing in the morning before you've brushed your teeth. It only happens in the movies.

Madonna — Formerly known as the Virgin Mary. Contemporary edition is the Anti-Virgin.

Madras — The appearance of all of your clothes if your husband does the wash.

Mafia — Fun group during a family reunion. However, proceed with caution before fighting with Uncle Vinnie over the turkey leg.

Magnify — Ability public restroom mirrors have with wrinkles and pores.

Magnum — Amount of English Leather cologne worn to late 1960's high school prom.

Maid — Housewife who is bonded.

Maim — This must be done to women who say they enjoy kneading dough.

Maintenance — To a woman: Hair, nails, exercise, diet, facials, clothes, etc. To a man : An all-you-can-eat buffet.

Make — Do not allow your husband to associate with men whose wives "make" things. He might expect you to "make" something besides reservations.

Maladjustment — Forgo any hasty requests to look in a mirror if you hear your plastic surgeon use this word as you're waking up from the anesthetic.

Malaria — Preferable to dieting.

Malcontent — Spouse who complains about Hamburger Helper meals.

Malevolent — Nature of woman who "puts up" her own vegetables.

Malformation — Not a good "oh, by the way" comment from the doctor following your husband's vasectomy.

Mall — Utopia.

Manacle — Don't let your husband talk you into one of these instead of a tennis bracelet.

Manchu — Check into electrolysis if you are pointed out as the "one in the pink dress and the manchu."

Manipulation — It is an excellent idea for a young woman to major in this in college.

Mannequin — If you come home and find your husband in bed with another woman and he claims she is just a mannequin, club her over the head to be sure.

Manor — Before letting your husband talk you into this residential upgrade, make sure it doesn't have a prefix of *"Mobile."*

Mansion — How your soon-to-be ex-husband describes the one bedroom hovel you were left with in the divorce settlement.

Marathon — Your day to drive the kid's carpool.

Marmoset — Reconsider starting a family with your new husband if a lot of people resembling this monkey were seated on "his" side at the wedding.

Maroon — Scary feeling of abandonment on your day to have the baby sitting co-op at your house.

Marriage — Proof the "buddy system" only works about 5% of the time.

Mart — Retail establishments with this suffix generally should be avoided when looking for engagement rings.

Marsupial — The perfect setup. This animal gets to give birth to a being about the size of a pea and stick it in her pocket until she's in the mood to deal with it.

Martyr — Demeanor of man who has to get his own Kleenex during a minor head cold.

Mascara — Second only to a pulse in the big scheme of things.

Mascot — Upsetting to learn your son has spent six years in college learning to become one of these.

Masquerade — Distressing to learn that your invitation to this party was noted "come as you are."

Matron — No coincidence this rhymes with apron.

Mausoleum — Don't marry anyone who lists this as their previous address — you'll never get a good night's sleep.

Maximum — Extremely confining word when used in relation to your credit limit.

Meander — Your six-year-old's gait whenever you are in a hurry.

Mediocre — The ultimate most men strive for in their lovemaking skills.

Megaphone — Keep one handy if you need to obtain a guy's attention during the Super Bowl.

Melancholy — Overwhelming funk often attributed to your husband leaving and not taking the kids.

Melba — Insane toast.

Mellow — Word never found in the same sentence with your two-year-old's name.

Melodrama — This is an after-dinner performance which follows your request for one of the kids to do the dishes.

Memento — Think twice before accepting another dinner invitation from a date who requests the T-bone from your steak to remember the evening by.

Menagerie — Demand your betrothed be a little more specific when you ask him "how many children would you like to have?"

Mend — Don't waste your time! Get a new one!

Menial — The duties of everyone in the delivery room other than the one in stirrups.

Menopause — How about MENO-STOP entirely?

Mephistopheles — Stand firm if your mother-in-law suggests this family name for your first born.

Meringue — Total waste of time, sugar and air.

Mind — Something you've lost so many times its not worth looking for, anymore.

Mingle — Bad idea at a leper colony.

Mink — Only animal that hasn't made its way into your closet.

Minute — Unachievable amount of time a mother asks to have alone each day.

Misbehavior — The way you'd like to think of your daughter's obsession with shaving the hair off all of her dolls.

Miscalculate — The distance between your car and the other car resting on your hood.

Miscellaneous — Everything in your life other than what's in your cosmetic case.

Misconstrue — This whole "for better or for worse" thing.

Miscount — The days since you took your last birth-control pill. Whoops!

Misdemeanor — Second degree assault on a man who refers to the large slabs of fat hanging over his belt as "love handles."

Miser — Husband who plans for retirement rather than vacations.

Misery — Being married to a miser.

Misfit — A woman who claims she likes being pregnant.

Misinform — Tell your husband the salesclerk must have done this regarding the price of the dress on the MasterCard bill. You clearly remember her mentioning two less zeros.

Mismanage — What men often do with thinning hair. They become preoccupied with "swooping."

Misname — Anyone called Dwight, Lothar or Ferd.

Misplace — Try not to do this with the children while you are shopping. Mall security can get a little testy about it.

Misprint — Obviously, the words "Most likely to succeed" under your husband's yearbook picture.

Misrepresent — Dates who drive nice cars that turn out to be stolen.

Missile — The salt shaker you asked your son to pass at the dinner table.

Mission — Try not to believe the laundry has been designated by God to be yours.

Mistake — Telling a street panhandler to meet you back at your car after you've cashed your paycheck.

Mistress — Has fewer "bad hair days" than wife.

Moat — Would not stop a Jehovah's Witness.

Mob — Most aggressive group can be found at day-after-Christmas sales.

Mobile — Hang a festive one on your headboard — IT, at least, might hold your attention.

Moccasin — Rebellious choice of footwear by a man who does not want to "get all dressed up in a tuxedo!"

Modern — What your husband considers all the furniture manufactured A.D.

Mogul — At any time of day you will find more of them on the ski slopes than in the boardrooms.

Monastery — Excellent place to find a husband. Make sure he is willing to keep his vow of silence.

Monophobia — Due to the close proximity of some member of your family at all times, they mistakenly believe you have this fear of being alone.

Monsoon — Small print on travel brochures of all of your tropical vacations.

Mooch — Neighbor who borrows sugar and your husband.

Mood — Totally based on consumption rate of chocolate.

Morbid — When your children start dividing up their inheritance at the dinner table.

Morphine — Conspicuously absent during childbirth.

Mortician — Occupation of mom on Thanksgiving morning as the Turkey awaits her on the slab/counter.

Mortify — Do this to your teenage daughter by chaperoning the Homecoming dance and wearing a dress identical to hers.

Mosaic — Explain this as the "look" you were going for when you drove your car through the plate glass window.

Mountie — Before you consider marrying one, ask yourself: "Am I really prepared to give this answer when someone asks me about my husband's occupation?"

Mud — Contrary to popular belief, does not require dirt and water. Merely requires the presence of children.

Mumbo Jumbo — Mechanic's well-rehearsed description of what is wrong with your car.

Mummy — Don't let the kids do this with deceased pets in order to get "extra credit" in science.

Museum — You might want to update your interior decorating if unexpected guests keep showing up at your house for tours.

Mustache — Negligent grooming tactic which is considered nonetheless more attractive on a man than a woman.

Mute — Your husband at a jewelry auction.

Mutiny — Situation which develops when trying to decide who's going to share their room with Grampa while he's in town for the Shriner convention.

Mutt — Don't name your son this — it isn't a name that "grows" up well.

Muzzle — Should be mandatory for all movie patrons who have been guilty of saying "Watch, here's the part where. . ."

THE **N** COLLECTION

Naive — Whoever came up with the "till death do us part" theory.

Nap — Unwise to do this at speeds exceeding 35 mph

Narrator — Singular ambition of person behind you during a suspense movie. See Muzzle.

Narrow — The line of sanity a mother walks on an hourly basis.

Nautical — Seek "power of attorney" when husband suggests leaving his six figure job to open up a "Nautical Shop" in Scottsbluff, Nebraska.

Neck — If you and a turkey have this in common immediately seek out a Plastic Surgeon.

Neglect — What the kids accuse you of if you are 30 seconds late picking them up.

Negotiate — Never suggest to the highway patrol that you'll take the ticket if he'll take the kids.

Neon — Make sure you and the kids are bonding properly if they all have flashing "for rent" signs in their bedroom windows.

Nepotism — Leave this off your resumé if this is the only reason you have ever been hired by anyone.

Nest — Don't let yourself get involved with a man who longingly refers to his parent's home in this manner.

Net — If your husband begins wrapping his hair in toilet paper at night and wearing one of these in the hot tub — it is grounds for divorce.

Neuter — Practice on the cat before attempting same with your husband.

Next — Waiting room summons in gynecologist's office which creates a spasm in your stomach.

Nice — When your teenage daughter speaks to you in this tone, be prepared to spend a lot of money.

Nifty — Think about getting a slightly older lover if, after sex, yours says "Man that was *nifty!*"

Nit-wit — Schedule a conference with your child's teacher if this keeps appearing on his evaluation forms.

Nobody — A twelve step self-esteem program might be in order if this is how you keep spelling your name.

Nomad — Luggage makes an excellent graduation gift if your son has chosen this career path.

Non-descript — Excellent way to describe your missing husband to the police — it could add years to the search.

Novocain — Would make a wonderful bath gel.

Now — Specific time frame in which your children expect their demands to be met.

Nudge — Maneuver often required to check husband's mortality at any event which doesn't center around a ball.

Numb — Reasonable request to make of doctor during labor.

THE O COLLECTION

Obituary — Exercise caution if the newspaper calls to check the correct spelling of your name for Thursday's column.

Object — Feel free to do this if your teenage kids continually borrow your panty hose to wear over their heads when they go out at night.

Oblivion — Good answer when your first grader asks what state their Dad was born in.

Obsess — Men tend to do this over dinner if it's not ready before 10:00.

Obsolete — Women who still get excited over a vacuum for their birthday.

Obvious — To a man : nothing.

Octogenarian — The last man who made a pass at you.

Oh — If this is your husband's response when you say you are leaving him, you have obviously waited too long.

Okay — Response typically given by spouse after you've spent six hours getting ready for a party and ask him "How do I look?"

Old — Most disturbing when your physician remembers you as his first grade teacher.

Olfactory — Most underdeveloped sense in males.

Omen — If your fiancé books a honeymoon suite for three at his mom's favorite hotel it should serve as a warning for the future of your marriage.

Omit — Suggest this be done with your weight on match-making service application if you haven't been out of your house since you stopped fitting through the front door.

Omnipresent — Kids.

Once — How many times it takes for a teenager to get pregnant.

Onlooker — Dad when the diaper needs changing.

Oodles — Not the answer you are seeking when asking your teenage daughter if she has ever had sex.

Ooze — Unappetizing way for the waiter to describe the sauce on your entrée.

Opaque — All glass surfaces with dogs or toddlers in the house.

Opinion — Usually offered without request by your teenage daughter regarding your hairstyle, clothing and parenting skills.

Opossum — Check around for another "gourmet club" if this fare keeps being served as the main course and the accompanying beverage is from a backyard still.

Optimistic — Outlook which has been foreign to your nature since your 6th child was born.

Opulent — How your mother-in-law describes your lifestyle since her son installed carpeting.

Orangutan — Unpleasant to look out your front window and discover the family moving in next door appears to have several of these with them.

Ordeal — Leaving husband in charge for one night out with the girls.

Organdy — Dump your husband immediately if he begins ordering custom suits made of this fabric.

Orgasm — Don't let him tell you this is just an "old wives tale."

Ostracize — If this continues happening to your family, begin eliminating them one by one until *you* are accepted.

Oija — Suggest your unemployed husband begin consulting the "Want Ads" as opposed to this form of job search.

Outburst — Can be offensive behavior during a funeral when laughing and cheering are involved.

Out-do — What every other woman has done at your high school reunion since you have the only husband who is serving time.

Outfit — In the case of most men, "uniform" would be the more appropriate description for the soiled T-shirt, jeans and Nikes.

Outing — If your husband does not return within 5 years, his absence can no longer be referred to in this manner.

Outline — Be ready with a good alibi if you return home to find a chalk rendering of your husband's body on the kitchen floor.

Out-live — Game played by elderly couples.

Oven — Can easily be converted to a cat box.

Overrule — Exercise this parental right if the kids suggest YOU move out when they turn 18.

Overtime — Any marriage that out-lasts the checking account.

Overweight — This applies to people whose cars are pulled over at truck weigh-in stations based solely on the appearance of the driver.

Oyster — Disgustingly slippery item which goes from your lips to your stomach with no swallowing involved.

THE **P** COLLECTION

Pact — Form one with the kids to drive their wealthy-but-tedious father insane.

Padlock — Subtle hint for hubby when one is attached to refrigerator door.

Page — Talk about good, clean fun... have your husband paged repeatedly when he is attending a sporting event with the "guys."

Pagoda — Find another architect if the one your husband hired specializes in this design only. Find an attorney if he wants to begin eating on the floor and for you to learn the art of massage.

Paint — A man's idea of re-modeling. Unfortunately, Sears Latex High-Gloss is available in an infinite number of brown shades.

Palace — What your husband accuses you of wanting just because you suggest an additional bathroom to the one which is presently serving your family of eight.

Pale — Sue your family physician if he says "I thought he looked a little pale last week during his checkup," when attending your husband's funeral.

Palimony — Seems to pay better than alimony.

Pall — This can befall a wedding reception when guests are informed it is a "cash bar."

Pamper — When your husband lets you sleep while making love.

Pandemonium — This breaks out when you suggest going out for dinner as opposed to the 5th day of turkey leftovers.

Pansy — Question your son's lifestyle if he says he really identifies with this flower.

Pantry — Seek another location for your children's time outs if they seem to be getting "chubby."

Paper mache`— Don't let contractor cut costs by using *this* for the exterior of your "dream home."

Parachutes — Subtle wedding gift from your friends encouraging you to "bail out" before it's too late.

Parade — Look into a weight loss program if you are continually being asked to participate as a float.

Paradise — Any hotel room where the Walton family isn't occupying the room above yours.

Parallelogram — Can be distracting if this is the shape of your blind date's head.

Paranoia — Chronic state of family ever since you started keeping the rat poisoning in your spice rack.

Par — More important to a golfer than world peace.

Paraphrase — Liberty your minister took with your marriage vows which later worked against you in the divorce settlement.

Parka — More realistic purchase for bride's trousseau than a peignoir.

Parsley — You may want to cook a couple of meals at home if your kids are invited to a friend's house for dinner and they won't eat because their plates are missing the *parsley* and orange slices.

Partridge — If you ever receive one in a pear tree as a Christmas gift, call the local authorities immediately and have your benefactor taken into custody.

Passive — Fire a divorce attorney who exhibits this temperament.

Paste — Not as good for hemming as a glue gun.

Pasteur — Some guy thinks to heat up a little milk and he's a genius. Women produce it and get no credit whatsoever!

Pastime — Use your gut instincts before hiring a yard man whose off hours are spent as a "Peeping Tom/Flasher."

Pasture — Husband's plans for the lawn because he's too lazy to mow it.

Patch — If both arms are covered with these and you still can't stop smoking, you'll probably be too "buzzed" to care.

Patio — What your husband calls the back part of your house since the walls collapsed.

Pawn-broker — Your oldest and dearest friend.

Peak — Disheartening to learn your new husband reached his during his first marriage.

Pedestal — If you want one, you're going to have to build it yourself.

Pedigree — If the dog's got to have one, shouldn't your husband?

Peek — Be leery of a man who asks you not to do this when he's undressing. Did you see the movie *Crying Game?*

Pelt — Avoid a furrier who used discarded toupees for his Fall line.

Penicillin — Do a background check if your date takes an inordinate amount of this medicine.

Peninsula — Shape of most men's hairline after forty.

Penthouse — Don't let a property rental agency convince you this and an attic are one in the same.

Pentothol — Lace a little of this through Grandma's cookies at the quilting bee — it will encourage "nap" time.

Per annum — Dusting schedule for realistic housewife.

Perch — Can be frightening to wake up and discover a buzzard roosting on your headboard based on the activity level of your husband.

Period — The end of a grammatical sentence and the beginning of a woman's sentence.

Perplex — Asking your husband the ages of your two children.

Personify — Futile attempts have been made by Al Gore.

Pessimistic — Nagging feeling of parents when their child's role model is the star of "The Bad Seed."

Petition — Consider moving if your neighbors have all signed this in an attempt to have your children institutionalized.

Petrify — Look into a makeover if child puts "What Mom does to my friends" as the definition for this word on his vocabulary test.

Pee-Wee — If this is nick-name of your fiancé, do some checking around before the wedding to find out how the name got started.

Phew — Can cause impotence if this is all wife has to say when lovemaking is over.

Pillow — Hard, lumpy sleep inhibitor used by Hotels to make sure you are up and ready to check out on time.

Pimp — Most Ivy League schools will immediately disqualify your son's application if he lists this as his father's line of work.

Pioneer — First male member of your family to gain employment outside of the prison laundry.

Pirouette — Can be a real "turn off" when husband twirls on his toes from the bathroom to the bed in this manner.

Pistol — Keep this weapon in night stand if husband continues to pirouette.

Pit — If your therapy group continues to refer to your home in this manner suggest they find another location for their sessions.

Plague — You might want to look for another day-care facility if this sign keeps popping up in their front window.

Plan — An obvious omission in my life.

Plaster — Shade of makeup preferred by most women over 40.

Plateau — An underachievers dream.

Platypus — Pet stores seem to always be out of these at Christmas.

Pliers — Register a complaint with the A.M.A. if your Ob-gyn has a tool belt filled with these strapped around his waist.

Plod — Unkind rumors can run rampant among the wedding guests if this is the pace of the groom.

Plot — Don't let your husband convince you that this 3 x 6 x 6 piece of real estate is Hallmark's recommendation for a 25th anniversary gift.

Polka — Do not perform this wedding ritual with a fat guy who isn't wearing a belt and tends to sweat a lot.

Poltergeist — Inexpensive sitter for the kids.

Pompadour — Hair style which has been rediscovered by the woman who takes the theater seat in front of you.

Poodle — Animal which requires more maintenance than you and will only ride in luxury cars.

Porcupine — These pelts would make excellent purses in high crime areas.

Porridge — Serve this instead of Fruit Loops, and your kids will have you brought up on abuse charges.

Portable — In the distorted world of people who camp — everything!

Posterior — Part of anatomy women are always checking in the mirror to assess all angles in all outfits.

Posthumous — Your biggest fear that this will be the only time you receive any recognition.

Pow-Wow — The gap between you and your teen will only widen if you insist on one of these every Saturday night.

Practice — First husbands.

Prairie — Probably not a good place to settle if you're single and over thirty.

Prance — If your husband begins to do this around the house hire a detective and have him followed.

Prank — Leaving town when your parents come to visit.

Preamble — Tiresome set-up given by husband for why you can't afford new furniture.

Propaganda — Diet books.

Prophylactic — Check quality control of your husband's brand if they have named a wing in obstetrics after you.

Psychedelic — Oddly, this look continues to prevail on golf courses.

Ptomaine — Avoid recipes which contain large amounts of this ingredient.

Pulse — Not a requirement for sitting in a golf gallery.

Puma — Can be a difficult house pet — impossible to keep it off the table if meat is being served.

Puke — Far too nice of word for "morning sickness."

Punctual — The timely manner in which one of your children barfs five minutes before your plane's departure.

Pygmy — Try to dissuade your daughter from marrying a member of this race — you can never get both families in the wedding pictures at the same time.

Pyramid — Can be disheartening if dressmaker suggests she won't need you present for fittings since she has a large cardboard triangle which can be used in your absence.

Pyromaniac — Keep the matches out of reach especially if this is the only word your child got right on the spelling test.

THE Q COLLECTION

Quack — Noise you soon regret teaching the baby.

Qualm — Uneasy feeling which accompanies a News Bulletin on television which begins with a close-up of your house.

Quarry — You have every right to be offended if family suggests dinner you slaved over tastes like it came from this area north of town.

Quest — Your search for a life.

Quibble — Silly argument involving the balance in the checking account.

Quiet — State of the room when you ask for volunteers to haul Grandma to the podiatrist.

Quilt — Only people with the patience to eat pomegranates have what it takes to be successful at making one of these.

THE **R** COLLECTION

Rabble — Offensive term your husband uses in regard to *your* side of the family.

Rabies — Disease your Cocker Spaniel picked up from the neighbor's kid.

Radiant — Last time you felt this way was after an X-ray.

Radical — The concept of your family members actually bending over to pick up various debris they have strewn throughout the house.

Raid — P.M.S. maneuver which leaves no cupboard untouched or refrigerator bin unexplored.

Raisin — If you have a rabbit for a family pet don't eat any of these just laying around the house.

Ramble — When your husband begins doing this through Sorority Houses, have him put to sleep.

Ramrod — Don't expect a lucrative career as a Proctologist if this is your last name.

Rascal — Description of son by parents in denial as he awaits his turn in the gas chamber.

Ration — Must be done with the groceries so you can afford to get your nails done.

React — Performance which must take place after husband's first orgasm if he has the energy to do it again.

Ream — Amount of toilet paper used by children during potty training. Or, amount of toilet paper used to fill a bra in Junior High.

Reason — Thinking skill found to be absent in people with tattoos.

Reassure — It is important to do this with remaining guests after the first guest in your buffet line has been taken out on a stretcher.

Rebirth — Unfortunately, this option is not available if you don't like the footage your husband captured on the video taping of your child's delivery.

Recede — Condition causing men to re-seed.

Receptacle — Anything within a man's reach. Don't think about this too long, it'll make you sick.

Recipe — Beware the woman who keeps hers in the safe deposit box. She was either over-exposed to Aunt Bea or hails from Stepford.

Recline — Conspiracy by Lazy Boy (an underground hate group) to encourage men to spend all non-eating time in this position.

Recluse — What you become in your own home when relatives are visiting.

Recoil — What happens when you reach under the kid's bed to clean.

Reconstruct — What you do with the events which brought you to your seat on the family couch every single night since the honeymoon.

Recover — This cannot be done after childbirth.

Rectangle — Difficult face shape to work with even with the most talented of makeup artists.

Redistribute — What a woman's body arbitrarily does with lumps, boobs and derrieres.

Reimburse — Request this monetary atonement for time and expenses while dating a man who forgot to tell you he's married.

Relative — Title which apparently gives the bearer the right to behave any way he wants.

Relief — Overwhelming sensation when the detective tells you it isn't your son after all who has been flashing the nursing home residents next door.

Rendezvous — Lovely French term American men have replaced with "shack up."

Repair — Guy thing. Women prefer to "replace."

Repetition — Only way to insure the slightest chance your husband will remember your birthday.

Reproduce — This option should NOT be made available to everyone.

Resort — Watch out for the word "last" in small print preceding "resort" in the travel brochure.

Revenge — The nickname your parents have given your daughter.

Rhinestone — This is grounds for annulment in most states.

Riff - raff — The groom's family.

Rut — Three letter word which seems preferable to your present chaotic lifestyle.

THE **S** COLLECTION

Sagebrush — Don't let the landscaper talk your husband into this low maintenance plant instead of grass — be firm.

Sanctuary — Any location where no one screams "Mom!" every five minutes.

Sanity — Went about the same time as virginity.

Sap — You grew up thinking this was your Dad's first name.

Schizoid — Thirteen-year-old girls.

Scrap — Portion of dinner remaining by the time mom gets to the table.

Scrimp — This is what your beloved did when he booked you on a Windjammer Cruise instead of a "real" cruise where the ships have hot water and you have the will to live.

Scurvy — Show pictures of victims of this disease to the kids and watch 'em guzzle that orange juice.

Seance — Saturday night entertainment of your elderly parents since everyone else in their pinochle group has passed on.

Sedate — Reasonable request of baby-sitter who has been with your kids before.

Seersucker — A little too festive of fabric for burial clothing.

Sequel — All marriages after the first one.

Sew — Waste of time. Just hot glue it instead!

Shack — Heading your home is listed under in the Realtor's guide.

Shag — Scary form of floor covering. Usually found in avocado or orange and almost always occupying the same room with vinyl bean-bag chairs.

Shanghai — When 52-year-old spinster daughter is still living with you, you may have to go to this extreme to procure her a husband for her before she sucks what's left of your life out of you.

Shenanigan — The judge may frown on this defense when your son is accused of torching his high school.

Shock — The discovery that the surgeon who performed your husband's vasectomy was an impostor.

Shovel — Quicker than vacuuming.

Skip — Unattractive gait for a man.

Slobber — ONLY a mother ignores this and continues drinking from her glass after letting her toddler have a "sip."

Slag — Word invented by my son to describe the extra skin that fans out from your thighs when you are sitting down.

Sling — Don't bother wearing one to try to get out of doing the laundry . . . it'll wait.

Slouch — Unless you are dating a man over age 75, this posture should not be acceptable.

Slump — This is not a legitimate excuse for your husband not working for over 10 years.

Smile — Painful to maintain muscle control during a long receiving line. Equally difficult to maintain when your husband is face down in the punch bowl.

Snap — What happens to a mother's mind when all the kids are talking to her at once.

Sniper — Upsetting to open the morning paper and discover yet another family member has chosen this career path.

Solitaire — Pastime for men who insist on eating beans for most every meal.

Sorority — Final opportunity to giggle for days at a time and wear other people's clothes.

Sparse — The crowd at a Gary Lewis and the Playboy's revival concert.

Spectator — A mother's duty 99% of the time or whenever you hear "Mom, watch me!"

Speculum — One of the two most dreaded "S" words — the other is "stirrups."

Spit — Unladylike conduct which caused Miss Arkansas' pageant disqualification for three consecutive years.

Spontaneous — Laughter during sex!

Spud — Reconsider a second date with a man who orders "spuds and gravy" in a French restaurant. Or for that matter, if he uses the word "spud" for any reason.

Squint — It's pathetic if you have to do this while watching your husband undress.

Squirrel — Don't let your son play for a team which has this animal for its mascot. Rest assured it will do nothing for his self-esteem.

Stalemate — Can occur in the divorce court when neither party wants custody of the kids.

Stamina — Trait possessed by any parent who can play three consecutive games of "CandyLand."

Stampede — What takes place the minute you pull into the car dealership and are spotted by the salesmen.

Stare — Happens all too often when you take your kids out to eat in public.

Static — Atmospheric electricity that can turn your skirt into a panty girdle.

Sterile — Might explain why none of the kids look like your husband.

Stimulants — Diamonds, gold, designer clothes, exotic vacations by yourself.

Stooge — Scholarship dreams die when your high school senior has been unanimously voted "Stooge of the Year" by the faculty.

Strategy — Technique used to get shopping bags from trunk of car to closet without being noticed.

Strict — What your teenage daughter accuses you of being since you won't let her throw a co-ed slumber party.

Strychnine — If you overhear your husband whispering this word to the pharmacist, stay alert.

Submachine gun — Only effective way to keep people with more than 10 items out of the Express Lane.

Supernatural — Woman who is not chemically dependent on chocolate.

Surrogate — Why didn't you think of this BEFORE you got pregnant?

Suspicious — Any efforts made by your children to get along with each other.

Swank — Your husband refers to Mr. Steak restaurant in this manner because they bring the food to you as opposed to a buffet line.

Sympathy — The unmistakable look on people's faces when they glance through your wedding album.

THE **T** COLLECTION

Taboo — Any discussion of the steel plate in Uncle Bob's head.

Tambourine — Instrument in which you are very accomplished, however it has kept you from being invited to parties.

Tank — Perfect for your 16-year-old's first car.

Tardy — The man who was going to take you away from all this. . .

Tattoo — Should require a 10-day waiting period and a sanity hearing.

Taxidermist — If this is your spouse's occupation, do not let him bring his work home with him.

Television — Husband would rather turn this on than his wife.

Tenant — Must be evicted if she's single, attractive and it takes your husband over two hours to collect the rent.

Tent — One should never have to vacation in something where the walls are made of canvas.

Test — It would be so much less intimidating if they would just call it a PAP "quiz."

Thaw — Until this process takes place, you can't fix dinner or have sex.

Throne — a.k.a. the Lazy Boy recliner.

Throng — Only way to describe your in-laws at a Moonlight sale at K-Mart.

Tinder — The wedding album after the divorce.

Toss — Unkind suggestion made by family in regard to the entire dinner, not just the salad.

Tradition — Embarrassing custom your family has of putting up the Christmas tree on December 26th because the trees are free.

Translate — Mom must do this for Dad when the children attempt to speak to him.

Transplant — Predictable solution to male baldness: just move old stuff around instead of getting something new.

Travel — Alternative to having children.

Turkey — Don't you wish the Pilgrims would have feasted on hot dogs instead?

THE U COLLECTION

Ugly — Those big blue monkey butts.

Ukulele — Only drawback to a Hawaiian vacation.

Umbilical — Cord you would swear was never cut due to the constant close proximity of your four-year-old when you are on the phone.

Unacceptable — Any excuse your husband offers for driving off while you are still in the gas station rest room.

Uncomfortable — Being matched to your gynecologist by the computer dating service.

Unconscious — How Geraldo obtains guests for his show.

Unconvincing — All reasons your husband invents after forgetting the name of your only child.

Undermanned — A woman's prison.

Undomesticated — The 90's woman.

Unexplored — The possibility of men being injected with a drug that simulates the labor experience in them so they can be more sympathetic to their wives.

Unfair — Men don't have biological clocks, or any timepiece for that matter, when they're on the golf course.

Unfinished — If purchased in this condition, most likely it will remain in this condition.

Unfurl — Dad's dramatic opening of the Rand McNally map the night before the big family vacation.

Unnavigable — The route planned above.

Unoccupied — The seat next to Jack Kervorkian.

Unpremeditated — The decision to leave the house without the credit cards.

Unshackle — First request of baby-sitter when parents return home.

Untimely — Husband's orgasm while you're still brushing your teeth.

Upkeep — For women: haircuts, hair color, permanents, sculptured nails, aerobics and diets. For men: gas in the car.

Upright — Unusual position for all men following a Sunday afternoon dinner.

Utopia — A place where men are severely punished for all odors and noises they expel.

THE **V** COLLECTION

Vague — Now that you think of it; the description of your blind date.

Valet — Person your family has you confused with.

Vamoose — Impolite request by your host following dinner.

Van — Seemed like a good idea until you are "volunteered" to shuttle every one else's kid whose mom opted for a sports car.

Vat — If your beauty consultant suggests you purchase all concealer products in this container, you might want to go that extra step and get a face-lift.

Veil — Cheap alternative to cosmetic surgery.

Vermin — Do not present well as hors d'oeuvres.

Victrola — What Grandpa calls the stereo.

Vigil — Nocturnal pastime of parents with teenagers.

Viking — Dating service may tell you they don't have one available, but it's worth a try.

Vinyl — Should be a "no brainer" for carpet replacement if you have pets and children.

Virgin — You may reapply for this status if the only man you've been with is Michael Jackson.

Voodoo — Last time there was a doctor in the family tree, he specialized in this medicine.

THE **W** COLLECTION

Wad — Do this with the noodles for a unique presentation.

Waddle — What do ducks and pregnant women have in common?

Waist — Tough to shop off-the-rack if this measurement exceeds your bust and hip measurements.

Wake — Be extra cautious if you overhear your husband telling people what to bring to the reception following yours.

Walrus — Animal which bears a strong resemblance to your Aunt Georgia, when she's dressed to go out.

Wan — Estee Lauder's latest foundation shade for women who gave birth after age 40.

War — Men came up with this idea when they were too old to have tantrums but still didn't want to share.

Ward — Housing threat wife makes to her husband as she sees more and more similarities between him and his dad.

Wart — This is NOT a beauty mark! Get it removed for cryin' out loud!

Wave — Has not caught on with golf galleries yet.

Wax — Should be way down on your list for hair removal. Bikini wax kits should come with Valium.

Web — Condition of 3-year-old's feet when they finally agree to get out of the bath they screamed about taking, to begin with.

Wedge — This can literally be drawn between you and your best friend if she is sleeping with your husband.

Weevil — This is just an ugly word. It should be recalled.

Weigh — Nurse's favorite entertainment. Especially fun to announce patient's results loud enough to inform the entire waiting room.

Whey — Favorite edible of the Muffet family. May require sitting on a tuffet to capture the full experience.

Whim — Unsettling answer for Neurosurgeon to give when patient asks how he chose this particular field.

Whittle — Do a quick background check on your fiancé if he seems exceptionally skilled at sculpting bars of soap into the shape of a handgun.

Woofer — Guy part of the speaker. The girl's part is Tweeter.

Wrinkle — Which came first — linen or the wrinkle?

THE <u>X</u> COLLECTION

Xylophone — Instrument developed at the request of Daniel Webster so there would be a word beginning with X in his dictionary.

THE Y COLLECTION

Yacht — Boat with an attitude.

Ya'll — Term used by Southerners when they can't remember more than one person's name.

Yellow — "Safe" color invented for baby showers.

Yodel — Not a wise talent choice for Miss America competition.

Youth — You don't want it when you have it and you don't have it when you want it!

THE **Z** COLLECTION

Zap — What happens to your energy if your stash of Snickers has been discovered and confiscated.

Zealot — A woman who irons her husband's socks.

Zest — This enthusiasm may be missing from your life if you're married to a mortician who brings his work home with him.

Zero — Number of times most women have fantasized about dating a guy named Newt.

Zilch — Chances of having the Publisher's Clearing House Prize Patrol standing at your front door.

Zing — High pitched sound whizzing by your right ear which leads you to discover you are standing in front of the kid's dart board.

Zigzag — Don't attempt to allude a police officer by driving in this whimsical manner in a school zone.

Zillion — Number of times your kids will ask you "how much farther?" between your driveway and your destination.

Zit — Count on uncontrollable sobbing and screaming by your teenage daughter following the discovery of this chin ornament on Prom Night.

Zodiac — Guys, if your favorite pick up line still is, "What's your sign?" your horoscope should tell you to plan on a life of solitude.

Zombies — Men at black tie benefits.

Zone — Women, don't be bullied by a few orange cones designating a "No Parking" area — they are made of rubber, just run over them!

Zonk — Should be the name for all de-caffeinated products.

Zoo — Even an occasional visit here doesn't guarantee you'll recognize the difference between men and animals.

ABOUT THE AUTHOR

Cy DeBoer is a humorist and essayist who lives in Colorado with her husband, Bruce, and their two children, Ryan and Whitney.

Writing, family, friends, church, home, community volunteering and Alpha Hydroxy treatments are all that stand between her and "a much needed nap!"

138

TITLES BY CCC PUBLICATIONS

Retail $4.99
30 – DEAL WITH IT!
40 – DEAL WITH IT!
50 – DEAL WITH IT!
60 – DEAL WITH IT!
OVER THE HILL – DEAL WITH IT!
RETIRED – DEAL WITH IT!
"?" book
POSITIVELY PREGNANT
WHY MEN ARE CLUELESS
CAN SEX IMPROVE YOUR GOLF?
THE COMPLETE BOOGER BOOK
FLYING FUNNIES
MARITAL BLISS & OXYMORONS
THE VERY VERY SEXY ADULT DOT-TO-DOT BOOK
THE DEFINITIVE FART BOOK
THE COMPLETE WIMP'S GUIDE TO SEX
THE CAT OWNER'S SHAPE UP MANUAL
PMS CRAZED: TOUCH ME AND I'LL KILL YOU!
RETIRED: LET THE GAMES BEGIN
THE OFFICE FROM HELL
FOOD & SEX
FITNESS FANATICS
YOUNGER MEN ARE BETTER THAN RETIN-A
BUT OSSIFER, IT'S NOT MY FAULT

Retail $4.95
YOU KNOW YOU'RE AN OLD FART WHEN...
1001 WAYS TO PROCRASTINATE
HORMONES FROM HELL II
SHARING THE ROAD WITH IDIOTS
THE GREATEST ANSWERING MACHINE MESSAGES OF ALL TIME
WHAT DO WE DO NOW?? (A Guide For New Parents)
HOW TO TALK YOU WAY OUT OF A TRAFFIC TICKET
THE BOTTOM HALF (How To Spot Incompetent Professionals)
LIFE'S MOST EMBARRASSING MOMENTS
HOW TO ENTERTAIN PEOPLE YOU HATE
YOUR GUIDE TO CORPORATE SURVIVAL
THE SUPERIOR PERSON'S GUIDE TO EVERYDAY IRRITATIONS
GIFTING RIGHT

Retail $5.95
THE BOOK OF WHITE TRASH
THE ART OF MOONING
GOLFAHOLICS
WHY GOD MAKES BALD GUYS
LOVE DAT CAT
CRINKLED 'N' WRINKLED
SMART COMEBACKS FOR STUPID QUESTIONS
YIKES! IT'S ANOTHER BIRTHDAY
SEX IS A GAME

SEX AND YOUR STARS
SIGNS YOUR SEX LIFE IS DEAD
40 AND HOLDING YOUR OWN
50 AND HOLDING YOUR OWN
MALE BASHING: WOMEN'S FAVORITE PASTIME
THINGS YOU CAN DO WITH A USELESS MAN
MORE THINGS YOU CAN DO WITH A USELESS MAN
THE WORLD'S GREATEST PUT-DOWN LINES
LITTLE INSTRUCTION BOOK OF THE RICH & FAMOUS
WELCOME TO YOUR MIDLIFE CRISIS
GETTING EVEN WITH THE ANSWERING MACHINE
ARE YOU A SPORTS NUT?
MEN ARE PIGS / WOMEN ARE BITCHES
THE BETTER HALF
ARE WE DYSFUNCTIONAL YET?
TECHNOLOGY BYTES!
50 WAYS TO HUSTLE YOUR FRIENDS ($5.99)
HORMONES FROM HELL
HUSBANDS FROM HELL
KILLER BRAS & Other Hazards Of The 50's
IT'S BETTER TO BE OVER THE HILL THAN UNDER IT
HOW TO REALLY PARTY!!!
WORK SUCKS!
THE PEOPLE WATCHER'S FIELD GUIDE
THE UNOFFICIAL WOMEN'S DIVORCE GUIDE
THE ABSOLUTE LAST CHANCE DIET BOOK
FOR MEN ONLY (How To Survive Marriage)
THE UGLY TRUTH ABOUT MEN
NEVER A DULL CARD
THE LITTLE BOOK OF ROMANTIC LIES
THE LITTLE BOOK OF CORPORATE LIES ($6.95)
RED HOT MONOGAMY (In Just 60 Seconds A Day) ($6.95)
HOW TO SURVIVE A JEWISH MOTHER ($6.95)
WHY MEN DON'T HAVE A CLUE ($7.99)
LADIES, START YOUR ENGINES! ($7.99)

Retail $3.95
NO HANG-UPS
NO HANG-UPS II
NO HANG-UPS III
HOW TO SUCCEED IN SINGLES BARS
HOW TO GET EVEN WITH YOUR EXES
TOTALLY OUTRAGEOUS BUMPER-SNICKERS ($2.95)

NO HANG-UPS – CASSETTES Retail $4.98

Vol. I:	GENERAL MESSAGES (Female)
Vol. I:	GENERAL MESSAGES (Male)
Vol. II:	BUSINESS MESSAGES (Female)
Vol. II:	BUSINESS MESSAGES (Male)
Vol. III:	'R' RATED MESSAGES (Female)
Vol. III:	'R' RATED MESSAGES (Male)
Vol. IV:	SOUND EFFECTS ONLY
Vol. V:	CELEBRI-TEASE